Further praise for Marie Howe
and *What the Living Do*

"The tentative transformation of agonizing, slow-motion loss into redemption is Howe's signal achievement in this wrenching second collection, which uncovers new potential for the personal poem."
—*Publishers Weekly* (starred review, and chosen as one of the five best books of poetry published in 1997)

"Her verse is almost unornamented though she manages through some great gift of will and expression to convey the sharpest feelings in long, graceful lines that seem to breathe on the page. . . . Despite the fathomless pain inherent in these poems, Howe never succumbs to sentimentality or self-pity; her tone is passionate yet detached, her vocabulary and imagery evocative, appropriate, and devastating."
—*Memphis Commercial Appeal*

"These are important poems by an established practitioner, defining contemporary poetry as accessible to all. . . . Howe is a truth-teller of the first order. Fearless in presenting unfiltered experiences, she interweaves her simple, economical language into long, subordinated sentences, loose, enjambed couplets that spill compellingly down the page with near-invisible artistry."   —*Providence Sunday Journal*

"The love in this book is tangible and redemptive."
—*Minneapolis Star Tribune*

"Marie Howe's poetry is luminous, intense, eloquent, rooted in abundant inner life."   —*Stanley Kunitz*

WHAT THE LIVING DO

WHAT
THE
LIVING
DO

p o e m s

Marie Howe

W. W. NORTON & COMPANY

NEW YORK · LONDON

For information about permission to reproduce selections from this book, write to Permissions,
W. W. Norton & Company, Inc., 500 Fifth Avenue, New York, NY 10110.

The text of this book is composed in Electra
with the display set in Electra Bold
Desktop composition by Chelsea Dippel
Manufacturing by The Courier Companies, Inc.
Book design by JAM Design

Library of Congress Cataloging-in-Publication Data

Howe, Marie, 1950–
What the living do : poems / Marie Howe.
p.   cm.
ISBN 0-393-04560-9
I. Title.
PS3558.O8925W48   1997
811'.54—DC21   97-10798
                                                                                                    CIP

ISBN 0-393-31886-9 pbk.

W. W. Norton & Company, Inc.
500 Fifth Avenue, New York, N.Y. 10110
www.wwnorton.com

W. W. Norton & Company Ltd.
Castle House, 75/76 Wells Street, London W1T 3QT

7 8 9 0

Some of these poems first appeared in *The Atlantic Monthly*; *Agni*; *Columbia Magazine*; the *Harvard Review*; the *New England Review*; the *Plum Review*; *Tikkun*; *Last Call: Poems on Alcoholism, Addiction & Deliverance* (edited by Sarah Gorham and Jeffrey Skinner); and *Lights, Camera, Poetry!: American Movie Poems* (edited by Jason Shinder).

"Practicing" and "The Fort" first appeared in *The New Yorker*.

I am grateful to the Bunting Institute at Radcliffe College, the Corporation of Yaddo, the Engelhard Foundation, the MacDowell Colony, and the National Endowment for the Arts for support: the time and space to work on these poems.

So many friends have helped me, too many to mention here, but I'm especially grateful to Marcus Alonso, who first walked me to the road, and to Charlene Engelhard for her many gifts and for walking with me.

I am grateful to Donna Masini for her generosity, and to my editor, Jill Bialosky, for her steady heart.

Finally, this book would not have come into being without the specific help I received from Jane Cooper, Tony Hoagland, Georgia Heard, James Shannon, and Jason Shinder.

Contents

With gratitude for my brother John Howe
in memory of Jane Kenyon and Billy Forlenza
and for the living, James Shannon.

WHAT THE LIVING DO

The Boy

My older brother is walking down the sidewalk into the suburban
   summer night:
white T-shirt, blue jeans—to the field at the end of the street.

Hangers Hideout the boys called it, an undeveloped plot, a pit
   overgrown
with weeds, some old furniture thrown down there,

and some metal hangers clinking in the trees like wind chimes.
He's running away from home because our father wants to cut his hair.

And in two more days our father will convince me to go to him—you know
where he is—and talk to him: No reprisals. He promised. A small parade
   of kids

in feet pajamas will accompany me, their voices like the first peepers
   in spring.
And my brother will walk ahead of us home, and my father

will shave his head bald, and my brother will not speak to anyone the next
month, not a word, not *pass the milk*, nothing.

What happened in our house taught my brothers how to leave, how to walk
down a sidewalk without looking back.

I was the girl. What happened taught me to follow him, whoever he was,
calling and calling his name.

Sixth Grade

The afternoon the neighborhood boys tied me and Mary Lou Mahar
to Donny Ralph's father's garage doors, spread-eagled,
it was the summer they chased us almost every day.

Careening across the lawns they'd mowed for money,
on bikes they threw down, they'd catch us, lie on top of us,
then get up and walk away.

That afternoon Donny's mother wasn't home.
His nine sisters and brothers gone—even Gramps, who lived with them,
gone somewhere—the backyard empty, the big house quiet.

A gang of boys. They pulled the heavy garage doors down,
and tied us to them with clothesline,
and Donny got the deer's leg severed from the buck his dad had killed

the year before, dried up and still fur-covered, and sort of
poked it at us, dancing around the blacktop in his sneakers, laughing.
Then somebody took it from Donny and did it.

And then somebody else, and somebody after him.
And then Donny pulled up Mary Lou's dress and held it up,
and she began to cry, and I became a boy again, and shouted Stop,

and they wouldn't.
And then a girl-boy, calling out to Charlie, my best friend's brother,
who wouldn't look

Charlie! to my brother's friend who knew me
Stop them. And he wouldn't.
And then more softly, and looking directly at him, I said, Charlie.

And he said Stop. And they said What? And he said Stop it.
And they did, quickly untying the ropes, weirdly quiet,
Mary Lou still weeping. And Charlie? Already gone.

The Fort

It was a kind of igloo
made from branches and weeds, a dome
with an aboveground tunnel entrance
the boys crawled through on their knees,
and a campfire in the center
because smoke came out of a hole in the roof,
and we couldn't go there. I
don't even remember trying, not
inside. Although I remember
a deal we didn't keep—so many
Dr Peppers which nobody drank,
and my brother standing outside it
like a chief: bare-chested, weary
from labor, proud, dignified,
and talking to us as if we could never
understand a thing he said because
he had made this thing and we had not,
and could not have done it, not
in a thousand years—true knowledge
and disdain when he looked at us.
For those weeks the boys didn't chase us.
They busied themselves with patching
the fort and sweeping the dirt outside
the entrance, a village of boys
who had a house to clean, women
in magazines, cigarettes and soda and
the strange self-contained voices they used
to speak to each other with.
And we approached the clearing where

their fort was like deer in winter
hungry for any small thing—what
they had made without us.
We wanted to watch them live there.

From My Father's Side of the Bed

When he had fallen deep asleep and was snoring
and I had moved out slowly from under his heavy arm,

I would sometimes nudge him a little,
not to wake him—

but so that he would sleep more lightly
and wake more easily should the soldiers,

maybe already assembling in the downstairs hall,
who were going to kill my father and rape my mother,

begin to mount the stairs.

Buying the Baby

In those days you could buy a pagan baby for five dollars,
the whole class saved up. And when you bought it

you could name it Joseph, Mary, or Theresa, the class took a vote.
But on the day I brought in the five dollars

my grandmother had given me for my birthday something happened
—a fire drill? an assassination? And if it was announced

Marie Howe has, all by herself, bought a baby in India and gets to name it,
it was overshadowed and forgotten.

And if I tried to picture my baby, the CARE package
carried to her hut and placed before her, as her sisters and brothers
    watched,

that image dissolved into the long shining hall to the girls' lavatory.
Even in my own room, waiting for Roy Orbison to sing "Only the Lonely"

so I could sleep, I couldn't conjure that baby up.
The five dollars I gave her would never reach her. I knew that:

because I wanted my class to think me good for giving it.
Spiritual Pride the nuns called it, a Sin of Intention,

sister to the Sin of Omission, which was
the price for what you hadn't done but thought.

Sometimes I prayed so hard for God to materialize at the foot of my bed it would start to happen;

then I'd beg it to stop, and it would.

Practicing

I want to write a love poem for the girls I kissed in seventh grade,
a song for what we did on the floor in the basement

of somebody's parents' house, a hymn for what we didn't say but thought:
That feels good or *I like that*, when we learned how to open each other's
    mouths

how to move our tongues to make somebody moan. We called it
    practicing, and
one was the boy, and we paired off—maybe six or eight girls—and
    turned out

the lights and kissed and kissed until we were stoned on kisses, and
    lifted our
nightgowns or let the straps drop, and, Now you be the boy:

concrete floor, sleeping bag or couch, playroom, game room, train
    room, laundry.
Linda's basement was like a boat with booths and portholes

instead of windows. Gloria's father had a bar downstairs with stools
    that spun,
plush carpeting. We kissed each other's throats.

We sucked each other's breasts, and we left marks, and never spoke of it
    upstairs
outdoors, in daylight, not once. We did it, and it was

practicing, and slept, sprawled so our legs still locked or crossed, a hand
   still lost
in someone's hair . . . and we grew up and hardly mentioned who

the first kiss really was—a girl like us, still sticky with the moisturizer we'd
shared in the bathroom. I want to write a song

for that thick silence in the dark, and the first pure thrill of unreluctant
   desire,
just before we made ourselves stop.

The Mother

In her early old age the mother's toenails curl over her toes
so that when she walks across the kitchen floor some click.

The doctor has warned her, for the third time, that her legs will
ulcerate if she doesn't rub moisturizer into them so

unwilling is she to touch her own body or care for it
—the same woman who stood many nights at the foot of that attic stairs

as her husband weaved and stammered up into the room where her
    daughter slept
—on the landing, in her bathrobe,

by the laundry chute, unmoving,
like a statue in the children's game her children play—

and now the soft drone of her daughter's waking voice, reasoning and
rising, and the first slap

and the scrape of her son's chair pushed back from his desk,
the air thick now with their separate listening,

and again the girl's voice, now quietly weeping, and the creak of her bed . . .
In the game, someone has to touch you to free you

then you're human again.

In the Movies

When a man rapes a woman because he's a soldier and his army's won,
there's always somebody else holding her down, another man,

so the men do it together, or one after the other,
in the way my brothers shot hoops on the driveway with their friends

while we girls watched. Their favorite game was PIG.
A boy had to make the exact shot as the boy before him, or he was a P

I G consecutively until he lost. I've been thinking
about the sorrow of men, and how it's different from the sorrow

of women, although I don't know how —

In the movies, one soldier holds the woman down, his hand over her mouth,
and another soldier or two holds down the husband

who's enraged and screaming because he can't help the woman he loves.
When the soldiers go, he crawls across the dirt and grass

to reach his wife who's speaking gibberish now.
He kisses her cheek over and over again . . .

—The woman lives on. We see her years later,
answering a man's questions in the drawing room, a crescent scar

just above her lace collar. She's dignified and serene. Maybe
her son has been recently killed, maybe she's successfully

married her daughter.
How can a woman love a man? In the movies, a man

rapes a woman because he's a soldier and his army's won, and he
wants to celebrate—all those nights in the dark and the mud—

and there's always someone else holding her down, another soldier, or
a friend, so the men seem to do it together.

The Attic

Praise to my older brother, the seventeen-year-old boy, who lived
in the attic with me an exiled prince grown hard in his confinement,

bitter, bent to his evening task building the imaginary building
on the drawing board they'd given him in school. His tools gleam

under the desk lamp. He is as hard as the pencil he holds,
drawing the line straight along the ruler.

Tower prince, young king, praise to the boy
who has willed his blood to cool and his heart to slow. He's building

a structure with so many doors it's finally quiet,
so that when our father climbs heavily up the attic stairs, he doesn't

at first hear him pass down the narrow hall. My brother is rebuilding
the foundation. He lifts the clear plastic of one page

to look more closely at the plumbing,
—he barely hears the springs of my bed when my father sits down—

he's imagining where the boiler might go, because
where it is now isn't working. Not until I've slammed the door behind

the man stumbling down the stairs again
does my brother look up from where he's working. I know it hurts him

to rise, to knock on my door and come in. And when he draws his
    skinny arm

around my shaking shoulders,

I don't know if he knows he's building a world where I can one day
love a man—he sits there without saying anything.

Praise him.
I know he can hardly bear to touch me.

Beth

I was going to sleep downstairs in the room we still called
The New Addition,

the wide bed the beat-up couch pulled out into
made me feel safe and glamorous under the dimmed yellow lights,

when my sister Beth came in quietly to tell me
she was going to the secret field to meet Rusty,

so that somebody would know in case anything happened.
And I half waited for her in the dim dark,

and passed the hour she promised to be back in gazing through
the open New Addition doors to the pool-yard's moonlight and water,

almost sleeping when she walked in hours later, still shaking
from the snarling dog that had chased her bike down the wide and empty
    avenue . . .

Her warm weight pulled the bed off center when she sat to tell me,
—the scent of that summer night pressing in through the screen doors,

the crickets lightly shaking their salt,
and my sister, still terrified and radiant, just come from Rusty's kisses—

I remember thinking: This is Beth
knowing her face in the dimness so well, feeling proud of her beauty,

so brave to have gone that far alone for him.
How had she learned to love a boy like that, without irony or
  condescension?

The Fruit Cellar

My father's tools were there:
hammers hanging from nails by their heads
and saws of diminishing sizes mounted on the wall

like the heads of small animals.
A vise screwed into the end of the battered worktable,
and in the air, the scent of sweet old sawdust,

although I never saw anybody work there.
Above the table, inside the wooden cupboards,
rows and rows of ketchups and mustards and mayonnaise,

family-sized tubs of peanut butter, family-sized jars of jam,
dozens of Campbell soups *lined up like soldiers*
and the cans of fruit cocktail my father had loved best in the war.

Dark in the corners, and darker inside the wooden bins
half filled with onions and potatoes.
The little kids were afraid to go down there.

Someone had to stand at the top of the laundry room stairs
and keep them talking, the way they do in coal mines
when the rescue is narrow and long. The thump of overhead

footsteps was no comfort, reaching into the fathomless bins.
That sound belonged to the lamplit world
carpeted with instructions and conversations,

and would disappear forever if the door accidentally shut.
Too far from the kitchen to be heard or found,
you had to climb up on the table and reach in blind for the jar,

scraping your knees getting up and down.
But I loved it there, late afternoons, no need to be accounted for,
I'd gaze at our family's store of supplies

and settle behind the door where my father's trunk sat,
opening it with a little internal ceremony
and read the letters other girls had sent him during the war,

earnest, sexless letters that they might have written in groups,
as women roll bandages, all chatting together—
girls I knew as Mrs. McDermott, and Mrs. Dollinger,

women who'd married my father's friends, interchangeable
as the blue ink on blue tissue paper written
in the convent school script I was supposed to be learning.

—one or two letters from my mother, years from knowing
she would marry him. For last I'd save the sword my father said
he'd stolen from a dead Japanese soldier,

but even then I knew he hadn't. And I'd lay the lie, curved a little
and still shiny, across my lap like a secret, unrecoverable history,
touching the blade lightly.

Then I'd return it,
return the letters, close the trunk
and carry what I'd come for back upstairs.

The Copper Beech

Immense, entirely itself,
it wore that yard like a dress,

with limbs low enough for me to enter it
and climb the crooked ladder to where

I could lean against the trunk and practice being alone.

One day, I heard the sound before I saw it, rain fell
darkening the sidewalk.

Sitting close to the center, not very high in the branches,
I heard it hitting the high leaves, and I was happy,

watching it happen without it happening to me.

The Game

And on certain nights,
maybe once or twice a year,
I'd carry the baby down
and all the kids would come
all nine of us together,
and we'd build a town in the basement

from boxes and blankets and overturned chairs.
And some lived under the pool table
or in the bathroom or the boiler room
or in the toy cupboard under the stairs,
and you could be a man or a woman
a husband or a wife or a child, and we bustled around
like a day in the village until

one of us turned off the lights, switch
by switch, and slowly it became night
and the people slept.

Our parents were upstairs with company or
not fighting, and one of us—it was usually
a boy—became the Town Crier,
and he walked around our little sleeping
population and tolled the hours with his voice,
and this was the game.

Nine o'clock and all is well, he'd say,
walking like a constable we must have seen
in a movie. And what we called an hour passed.

Ten o'clock and all is well.
And maybe somebody stirred in her sleep
or a grown up baby cried and was comforted . . .
Eleven o'clock and all is well.
Twelve o'clock. One o'clock. Two o'clock . . .

and it went on like that through the night we made up
until we could pretend it was morning.

The Girl

So close to the end of my childbearing life
without children

—if I could remember a day when I was utterly a girl
and not yet a woman—

but I don't think there was a day like that for me.

When I look at the girl I was, dripping in her bathing suit,
or riding her bike, pumping hard down the newly paved street,

she wears a furtive look—
and even if I could go back in time to her as me, the age I am now

she would never come into my arms
without believing that I wanted something.

The Dream

I had a dream in the day:
I laid my father's body down in a narrow boat

and sent him off along the riverbank with its cattails and grasses.
And the boat—it was made of bark and wood bent when it was wet—

took him to his burial finally.
But a day or two later I realized it was my self I wanted

to lay down, hands crossed, eyes closed. . . .
Oh, the light coming up from down there,

the sweet smell of the water—and finally, the sense of being carried
by a current I could not name or change.

For Three Days

For three days now I've been trying to think of another word for
   gratitude
because my brother could have died and didn't,

because for a week we stood in the intensive care unit trying not to
   imagine
how it would be then, afterwards.

My youngest brother, Andy, said: This is so weird. I don't know if I'll be
talking with John today, or buying a pair of pants for his funeral.

And I hated him for saying it because it was true and seemed to tilt it,
because I had been writing his elegy in my head during the seven-hour
   drive there

and trying not to. Thinking meant not thinking. It meant imagining my
   brother
surrounded by light—like Schrödinger's Cat that would be dead if you
   looked

and might live if you didn't. And then it got better, and then it got worse.
And it's a story now: He came back.

And I did, by that time, imagine him dead. And I did begin to write
   the other story:
how the crowd in the stifling church snapped to a tearful attention,

how my brother lived again, for a few minutes, through me.
And although I know I couldn't help it, because fear has its own language

and its own story, because even grief provides a living remedy,
I can't help but think of that woman who said to him whom she
    considered

her savior: If thou hadst been here my brother had not died, how she
    might
have practiced her speech, and how she too might have stood trembling,

unable to meet the eyes of the dear familiar figure that stumbled from
    the cave,
when the compassionate fist of God opened and crushed her with
    gratitude and shame.

Just Now

My brother opens his eyes when he hears the door click
open downstairs and Joe's steps walking up past the meowing cat

and the second click of the upstairs door, and then he lifts
his face so that Joe can kiss him. Joe has brought armfuls

of broken magnolia branches in full blossom, and he putters
in the kitchen looking for a big jar to put them in and finds it.

And now they tower in the living room, white and sweet, where
John can see them if he leans out from his bed which

he can't do just now, and now Joe is cleaning. What a mess
you've left me, he says, and John is smiling, almost asleep again.

A Certain Light

He had taken the right pills the night before.
We had counted them out

from the egg carton where they were numbered so there'd be no
    mistake.
He had taken the morphine and prednisone and amitriptyline

and Florinef and vancomycin and Halcion too quickly
and had thrown up in the bowl Joe brought to the bed—a thin string

of blue spit—then waited a few minutes, to calm himself,
before he took them all again. And had slept through the night

and the morning and was still sleeping at noon—or not sleeping.
He was breathing maybe twice a minute, and we couldn't wake him,

we couldn't wake him until we shook him hard calling, John wake up now
John wake up—Who is the president?

And he couldn't answer.
His doctor told us we'd have to keep him up for hours.

He was all bones and skin, no tissue to absorb the medicine.
He couldn't walk unless two people held him.

And we made him talk about the movies: What was the best moment in
On the Waterfront? What was the music in *Gone with the Wind*?

And for seven hours he answered, if only to please us, mumbling
I like the morphine, sinking, rising, sleeping, rousing,

then only in pain again—but wakened.
So wakened that late that night in one of those still blue moments

that were a kind of paradise, he finally opened his eyes wide,
and the room filled with a certain light we thought we'd never see again.

Look at you two, he said. And we did.
And Joe said, Look at you.   And John said, How do I look?

And Joe said, Handsome.

How Some of It Happened

My brother was afraid, even as a boy, of going blind—so deeply
that he would turn the dinner knives away from, *looking at him,*

he said, as they lay on the kitchen table.
He would throw a sweatshirt over those knobs that lock the car door

from the inside, and once, he dismantled a chandelier in the middle
of the night when everyone was sleeping.

We found the pile of sharp and shining crystals in the upstairs hall.
So you understand, it was terrible

when they clamped his one eye open and put the needle in through
    his cheek
and up and into his eye from underneath

and left it there for a full minute before they drew it slowly out
once a week for many weeks. He learned to, *lean into it,*

to *settle down* he said, and still the eye went dead, ulcerated,
breaking up green in his head, as the other eye, still blue

and wide open, looked and looked at the clock.

My brother promised me he wouldn't die after our father died.
He shook my hand on a train going home one Christmas and gave me
    five years,

as clearly as he promised he'd be home for breakfast when I watched him
walk into that New York City autumn night. *By nine, I promise,*

and he was—he did come back. And five years later he promised five
  years more.
So much for the brave pride of premonition,

the worry that won't let it happen.
You know, he said, I always knew I would die young. And then I got sober

and I thought, OK, I'm not. I'm going to see thirty and live to be an old
  man.
And now it turns out that I am going to die. Isn't that funny?

—One day it happens: what you have feared all your life,
the unendurably specific, the exact thing. No matter what you say or do.

This is what my brother said: Here, sit closer to the bed
so I can see you.

Rochester, New York, July 1989

Early summer evenings, the city kids would ride their bikes down his
    street
no-handed, leaning back in their seats, and bump over the curb

of the empty Red Cross parking lot next door where Joe's car was
    parked, and
John's white Honda, broken and unregistered . . . everything blooming,

that darkening in the trees before the sky goes dark: the sweetness of the
    lilacs
and the grass smell . . .

And the sound on the front porch steps was wooden and hollow,
and up the narrow stairway stuffy and dim, and the upper door maybe a little

open—and into the hall and left into his room: someone might be sitting
    there
reading, or sometimes only him, sleeping,

or lying awake, his face turned toward the door,
and he would raise his hand. . . .

And the woman who lived below them played the piano. She was a
    teacher, and
sometimes we'd hear that stumbling repetition people make when they're

learning a new song, and sometimes she'd play alone—she'd left a note
in his mailbox saying she would play softly for him. And those evenings,

when the sky was sunless but not yet dark, and the birdsong grew loud
    in the trees,
just after supper, when the kids wheeled by silently

or quietly talking from their bikes, when the daylilies closed up
alongside the house,

music would sometimes drift up through the floorboards,

and he might doze or wake a little or sleep,
and whoever was with him might lean back in the chair beside the bed

and not know it was Chopin,
but something soft and pretty—maybe not even hear it,

not really, until it stopped
—the way you know a scent from a flowering tree once you've passed it.

The Last Time

The last time we had dinner together in a restaurant
with white tablecloths, he leaned forward

and took my two hands in his hands and said,
I'm going to die soon. I want you to know that.

And I said, I think I do know.
And he said, What surprises me is that you don't.

And I said, I do. And he said, What?
And I said, Know that you're going to die.

And he said, No, I mean know that you are.

Without Music

Only the car radio
driving from the drugstore to the restaurant to his apartment:

rock and roll, oldies but goodies,
and sometimes, softly, piano music

rising from the piano teacher's apartment on the first floor.

Most of it happened without music,
the clink of a spoon from the kitchen,

someone talking. Silence.

Somebody sleeping. Someone watching somebody sleep.

Pain

He rose on the surface of it like the layer of water on top of a wave
that won't break—you've seen those swells—

cold and moving like something breathing you can't see, collecting and
collecting until it seems uncontainable, heaving on and on, rising and

rising and growing bigger.
When it got very bad, he'd say, Tell me a story,

and after an hour or so, he'd say, We got through that one, didn't we?

Until a day came when he said, Marie,
you know how we've been waiting for the big pain to come?

I think it's here. I think this is it.
I think it's been here all along.

And he did take the morphine, and he died the next week.

Faulkner

During the last two weeks of John's life, Joe was reading
As I Lay Dying for his English class. He had to give an oral report,

and John kept asking me to read it. You're an English teacher, he said,
you know what they want. OK, I said. But the book drifted

from the kitchen to the bedside table to the pillows of the living room
   couch.
What's it about? I asked Joe, late one night

when we were making peanut butter sandwiches. But I didn't understand
the story as he told it: the good brothers from the bad brothers,

who was the mother's favorite, really? And who was building the coffin,
banging and banging the nails?

The afternoon John died, I picked it up, waiting for the food from the
   aunts
and the cousins. I tried to read it that night before I fell asleep

and stopped. I don't know what finally happened.
Caddy smelled of trees, I kept thinking during those days and nights

of the wake and the funeral. But that was another book, wasn't it?
That was the idiot brother talking.

The Promise

In the dream I had when he came back not sick
but whole, and wearing his winter coat,

he looked at me as though he couldn't speak, as if
there were a law against it, a membrane he couldn't break.

His silence was what he could not
not do, like our breathing in this world, like our living,

as we do, in time.
And I told him: I'm reading all this Buddhist stuff,

and listen, we don't die when we die. Death is an event,
a threshold we pass through. We go on and on

and into light forever.
And he looked down, and then back up at me. It was the look we'd pass

across the kitchen table when Dad was drunk again and dangerous,
the level look that wants to tell you something,

in a crowded room, something important, and can't.

The Cold Outside

Soon I will die, he said—that was during the heat wave that summer:
the orange lilies bending toward the house beside the driveway,

the heater in his car broken on, and blasting.
And the green shade flapped against the window screen,

as if what was out there inhaled and exhaled,
sliding away from the window, banging lightly against the sill

sucked flat against the screen
—peeling off and blowing out again.

Today the cold outside is bright and brittle,
heaps of hard snow between the sidewalk and the street,

and look, someone has shoveled a narrow path in front of the bakery,
so that, walking, a person has to step aside,

and let another person through,
or pass through as the other person steps aside.

Soon I will die, he said, and then
what everyone has been so afraid of for so long will have finally happened,

and then everyone can rest.

The Grave

That first summer I lay on the grass above it as if it were
a narrow bed, just my size, and—

lying on the ground above my brother's body like a log
floating on lake water above its own shadow.

*   *   *

During the first winter I drove there one afternoon
after Tom and Andy and Beth and Dor and Bahia had been there,

because when I stepped out of the car their footprints marked the
    snowy lawn:
the men's big boots, the women's smaller ones,

and Bahia's little boot prints, as big as my hand, looping and falling down
into a snow angel next to his grave, then another messy angel on it,

and, a grave or two away, another one, and the little blotch where she
    got up
and brushed herself off. For some crazy reason I was wearing

black high-heeled shoes in the snow, and, walking back to the car,
    they made
ovals and dots, fat exclamation marks,

walking inside the steps of my brothers and sisters.

＊　＊　＊

One November, years later, I went there with Andy
who was, by then, as old as John was when he died,

and we lay on the frozen ground,
I, using my scarf as a pillow, on John's grave,

and Andy, on top of our father's grave, one grave away,
and we talked like that for a little while, companionably,

like an old couple talking in bed,
our eyes closed against the sunlight,

and when I cried, Andy didn't seem to wish me to stop, and that
was a kind of happiness,

lying there with my living brother, talking about our family.
The ground was cold.

Eventually the chill crept through our coats and jeans and
we scuffled up—Andy reached down

to give me his hand—and then it was over.
We walked together back to the car and away from them.

The Gate

I had no idea that the gate I would step through
to finally enter this world

would be the space my brother's body made. He was
a little taller than me: a young man

but grown, himself by then,
done at twenty-eight, having folded every sheet,

rinsed every glass he would ever rinse under the cold
and running water.

This is what you have been waiting for, he used to say to me.
And I'd say, What?

And he'd say, This—holding up my cheese and mustard sandwich.
And I'd say, What?

And he'd say, This, sort of looking around.

One of the Last Days

As through a door in the air that I stepped through sideways
before reaching for a plate high in the cupboard

I find myself in the middle of my life: May night, raining,
Michael just gone to Provincetown, James making pizzas next door,

lilacs in full bloom, sweet in the dark rain of Cambridge.

On one of the last days I told him, You know how much you love Joe?
That's how much I love you. And he said, No. And I said, Yes.

And he said, No. And I said, You know it's true.
And he closed his eyes for a minute.

When he opened them he said, Maybe you'd better start looking for
somebody else.

Late Morning

I was still in my white nightgown and James had drawn me down
to sit on his lap, and I was looking over his shoulder through the hall

into the living room, and he was looking over my shoulder, into the trees
through the open window I imagine,

and we sat like that for a few minutes, without saying much of anything,
my cheek pressed lightly

against his cheek, and my brother John was dead.
Suddenly close and distinct, it seemed finished, as if time were a
  room

I could gaze clear across—four years since I'd lifted his hand from
the sheets on his bed and it cooled in my hand.

A little breeze through the open window, James's warm cheek,
a brightness in the windy trees as I remember, crumbs and dishes
  still

on the table, and a small glass bottle of milk and an open jar of
raspberry jam.

Wanting a Child

I want to write about God and suffering and how the trees endure
   what we
don't want—the long dead months before the appalling blossoms.

But I think about James instead,
how last night, when he stood in the doorway bare-chested, I leaned
   down and

pressed my cheek against his belly,
and drew the side of my face up over his chest, his shoulder and throat

and chin and cheek. I did it over and over again,
leaning down and dragging my cheek up against him.

Tonight Jane sleeps between white hospital sheets. She's already lost
   her hair
from treatment. Two more years of it: six months on, six months off,

I almost envy the simplicity of her life,
deprived of a certain future.

Snowy evening in a dark snowy winter:
daffodils in the glass vase on the mantel over the fireplace that doesn't work.

The radiator's squeak and whine.
Plows soon, their deep and decent rumbling. Then more night,

more snow and wind, and in the morning, somebody shoveling.

Tulips

The purple tulips I bought this week at the Evergood market
dip from their brown clay pot like little wolves

bringing their throats low to the table, their petals wide open.
They are so beautiful, I stand in the hallway a long time

looking at them. Who said: *Their face and their sex
is the same*, about tulips?

And when James comes through the door with his head bowed, when
he stands in the porch alone, smoking,

I tell him: Come into the living room and look at these tulips. And he does.
He sits down in the rocking chair, and he looks at them.

And when I say: Look how the gold from the stamen has fallen
to the inside of the purple petal, so the petal holds it,

he says, Yeah, I see that. But he's sad.

I think of my father and my brothers. I look at the tulips.
And James holds his head in his hands.

Watching Television

I didn't want to look at the huge white egg the mother spider dragged
along behind her, attached to her abdomen, held off the ground,

bigger than her own head —
and inside it: hundreds of baby spiders feeding off the nest,

and in what seemed like the next minute,
spinning their own webs quickly and crazily,

bumping into each other's and breaking them, then mending
and moving over, and soon they got it right:

each in his or her own circle and running around it.
And then they slept,

each in the center of a glistening thing: a red dot in ether.

Last night the moon was as big as a house at the end of the street,
a white frame house, and rising,

and I thought of a room it was shining in, right then,
a room I might live in and can't imagine yet.

And this morning, I thought of a place on the ocean where no one is,
no boat, no fish jumping,

just sunlight gleaming on the water, humps of water that hardly break.

I have argued bitterly with the man I love, and for two days
we haven't spoken.

We argued about one thing, but really it was another.
I keep finding myself standing by the front windows looking out at the
  street

and the walk that leads to the front door of this building,
white, unbroken by footprints.

Anything I've ever tried to keep by force I've lost.

The Dream

Jane's voice on the phone is grave and soft and strong.
Her hair's gone. I cut it off, she said. She's Joan of Arc now.

Dogs bark at people they don't know.
All those barking dogs in my dreams! And now

they know me and don't bark. A cat screams from the yard.
I'd live with you, but I wouldn't marry you, is what

my father said, offhandedly, from the couch.
He's dead now. And the sentence burns in my heart.

Jane's voice belongs to another world:
the world I entered when I decided to leave my father.

Sometimes the island wavers and shimmers underfoot,
but the bridge appears when you walk across it—that's

how it works, right? There's no end to this.

More

More snow falling, and the scrape of a shovel . . .
a layer of snow on top of the seeds in the feeder outside the porch
     window.

It looks like a geological map now: the little world in layers: water then silt
then rock. Wishing a rock into water doesn't work.

I can reach through the open window and scoop off the snow, scattering it
down the four stories with my hand.

But nothing I can do will hurry him or promise it. It might be hours
     or days
before he appears at the door and sits me down and lays his head in
     my lap.

Separation

Driving out of town, I see him crossing
the Brooks Pharmacy parking lot, and remember

how he would drop to his knees in the kitchen
and press his face to my dress, his cheek flat against

my belly as if he were listening for something.
Somebody might be waiting for coffee in the living room,

someone might be setting the dining room table, he'd
place his face under my dress and press his cheek

against my belly and kneel there, without saying anything.
How is it possible that I am allowed to see him

like this — walking quickly by the glass windows?

— what he wears in the world without me,
his hands swinging by his side, his cock quiet

in his jeans, his shirt covering
his shoulders, his own tongue in his mouth.

The Bird

Even when I held my hands over my ears
I could hear the sirens squealing down the avenue:

somebody else's trouble: broken or
bleeding or burned: and through the porch windows

a bird in the ash tree kept calling out: bleating,
like the hungry cry of a human child and wouldn't stop.

Even when I opened the window
and yelled at the bird, it bleated on

the way a child does when you shake it.
Down the four flights to the courtyard of the building

I could still hear it,
and around the corner to the mailbox: there too.

Cool Hand Luke finally said: Just don't hit me again Boss. Please
just don't hit me again.

And his men turned against him and spit in his food.
No attic anymore; no stumbling drunk, he's dead;

no belt; no pencil; no safety pin,
only a summer afternoon in a small city: porch windows,

bird singing. How many hands does a city have?
Yesterday each one was a sound.

And the bird's trouble? It must have gotten solved
—all that insistent complaint.

By the time I fell asleep, it was quiet.

Prayer

Someone or something is leaning close to me now
trying to tell me the one true story of my life:

one note,
low as a bass drum, beaten over and over:

It's beginning summer,
and the man I love has forgotten my smell

the cries I made when he touched me, and my laughter
when he picked me up

and carried me, still laughing, and laid me down,
among the scattered daffodils on the dining room table.

And Jane is dead,
                              and I want to go where she went,
where my brother went,

and whoever it is that whispered to me

when I was a child in my father's bed is come back now:
and I can't stop hearing:
                              This is the way it is,
the way it always was and will be—

beaten over and over—panicking on street corners,
or crouched in the back of taxicabs,

afraid I'll cry out in jammed traffic, and no one will know me or
know where to bring me.

                         There is, I almost remember,
another story:

It runs alongside this one like a brook beside a train.
The sparrows know it; the grass rises with it.

The wind moves through the highest tree branches without
seeming to hurt them.

Tell me.
Who was I when I used to call your name?

Two or Three Times

The two or three times my father tried to quit drinking,
for a few days

maybe a week,
he would walk carefully around the house, feeling his way

through the kitchen and the pantry.
His fingers trembled like a girl's.

And there was a light around him, fragile and already cracked
we could see clear through

which was his hope, which he shared with no one.

James looked like that yesterday,
standing outside on the step, the cardboard deli tray in his hands . . .

a bright cold morning, his eyes clear and blue.
And he was up early, and he'd brought coffee the way I like it

with a straw he must have dropped in the driveway,
and a raspberry Danish he placed on the paper plate with ceremony:

the red-seeded center sticky within the little swirly circle.

Reunion

The very best part was rowing out onto the small lake in a little boat:

James and I taking turns fishing, one fishing while the other rowed
   slowly—
the long sigh of the line through the air,

and the far plunk of the hook and the sinker—
lily pads, yellow flowers

the dripping of the oars
and the knock and creak of them moving in the rusty locks.

The Kiss

When he finally put
his mouth on me — on

my shoulder — the world
shifted a little on the tilted

axis of itself. The minutes
since my brother died

stopped marching ahead like
dumb soldiers and

the stars rested.
His mouth on my shoulder and

then on my throat
and the world started up again

for me,
some machine deep inside it

recalibrating,
all the little wheels

slowly reeling then speeding up,
the massive dawn lifting on the other

side of the turning world.
And when his mouth

pressed against my
mouth, I

opened my mouth
and the world's chord

played at once:
a large, ordinary music rising

from a hand neither one of us could see.

Yesterday

Just yesterday,
three days after my forty-fifth birthday,
a mild October afternoon,
somewhere around five o'clock,
and maybe the seventh or eighth time
I'd gone to check—

Now that it's happened, it seems it had to happen.

Still the house had built itself a corridor I'd been hurrying through
towards the sleeping child,

thinking of Sarah's angel, hearing Sarah's laugh.

The white curtains billowed slightly in the mild, October wind
—but there was no baby, and hadn't been.

Memorial

Michael took Billy's black leather jacket,
Richard took his Polaroid camera,

I'm not sure but I think Nick took a big rug.
Frances wrapped a belt around Nick's neck from behind

and said, I want this, can I have it?

I took the small white lamp, the green painted table
and the picture Billy had taken of the fish James said he'd caught

the afternoon he bought it from the fishermen
returning with their heavy silver boats at dusk.

.   .   .

Michael picked up the green vase and carried the ashes ahead, leading
us carefully along the icy spine of the dunes.

And when we arrived at the promontory place
and threw the ashes into the wind that blew some of them back into
      our faces,

I didn't think: This is Billy's bones and flesh, his eyes and mouth and
      cock,
I thought: Michael is taking charge when Billy said I was in charge of
      the ashes.

Jesus said, Mary chose the better part, to Martha, who was complaining
   about
her sister not helping. She never helped.

But I love that woman slamming around the kitchen. She's made
   food enough
for more than a dozen people, and no one's even the least bit hungry—

She's scraping the plates into a stack to carry to the table and now she
   sets them
down heavily with a huff. Jesus is speaking in a quiet voice.

He's a kind man, Martha is thinking: he doesn't mean any harm, but if I
   don't do it,
it won't get done.

.   .   .

—as Billy died,
the space between his breaths got bigger

and longer,

then three quick breaths
a little gurgling of breath and blood,

then a long silent space
—   and not another breath,

then one more,
        and that was it.

His sister weeping,

and something began to move through the room,
    as if energy were

rising, like thickening air,
    as if spirit were pleasure

pushing through the room, through
    even our faces,

a molecular, invisible . . .
    If this was Billy

he was so vast—
    the way one field leads onto another,

vast to have been contained,
    all that time, in that body,

—a nearly unendurable joy
    a steady outpouring for over an hour

so that when the men came back from dinner they found
    Billy dead in the sheets

and the three of us almost drunkenly smiling.

 ·   ·   ·

When James comes in from plowing for hours, stomping
his big boots by the open door, he's beautiful,

but I don't tell him that. I say: aren't you going to your music lesson?
Thinking: why don't you make more money?

When I tell him about post-modern brokenness in Caroline Forche's
    poems,
that can't be repaired, he stirs the old fire with a stick,

and reaches in with his hands and moves one log so it sits
on top of the other. Then I think: James is stupid,

he doesn't know that the personal narrative is obsolete. And I think
about how Billy used to call me Angel Face—

how after he died we found out that he called a lot of us that.
I don't know the meaning of my own life anymore, is what I tell James,

and he says, Yes you do. You've forgotten, but you'll remember again.
And when I stare at him steadily, he rises

from where he's crouching by the fire and leans over my chair,
and opens and closes his eyes so his lashes brush my throat and lips
    and cheek

I'm hungry, he says. What do you want to eat?

My Dead Friends

I have begun,
when I'm weary and can't decide an answer to a bewildering question

to ask my dead friends for their opinion
and the answer is often immediate and clear.

Should I take the job? Move to the city? Should I try to conceive a child
in my middle age?

They stand in unison shaking their heads and smiling—whatever leads
to joy, they always answer,

to more life and less worry. I look into the vase where Billy's ashes were—
it's green in there, a green vase,

and I ask Billy if I should return the difficult phone call, and he says, yes.
Billy's already gone through the frightening door,

whatever he says I'll do.

The Visit

Some fumbling,
turning it this way and that:

OK, here it is, the doctor said,
and there was the little tumor

of nerves or blood that ought not
to be there: my brain's upper right window,

a little face peeking out, a child
who won't go to bed: little knot of cells

little hairball on the sill,
Benign is what he said, as God is said to be,

but for a moment I still stood,
—I could almost feel it with my foot,

in the place where they had stood:
John and Jane and Billy.

Then I was in the corridor again,
it was Spring Street in February and raining,

and the negatives slipped into a plain brown envelope
so I could take them home with me.

The New Life

This morning, James still deep asleep under the embroidered white
   sheets
a heavy heavy rain

the city still dark and the rain so loud the city was quiet,
a shhhh in the streets, as I drove up First Avenue happy, from
   Twenty-first Street

to Fifty-seventh Street without a light to stop for, a deep privacy in the car,
and nobody, for once, beeping—

the sky behind the falling rain lightening from dark to heavy gray—
and why shouldn't I be happy, and why shouldn't we argue

and sit in the two kitchen chairs, our faces downcast, after I get home
after what we've done, what we have allowed ourselves to long for?

What the Living Do

Johnny, the kitchen sink has been clogged for days, some utensil probably
  fell down there.
And the Drano won't work but smells dangerous, and the crusty dishes
  have piled up

waiting for the plumber I still haven't called. This is the everyday we
  spoke of.
It's winter again: the sky's a deep headstrong blue, and the sunlight
  pours through

the open living room windows because the heat's on too high in here, and
  I can't turn it off.
For weeks now, driving, or dropping a bag of groceries in the street,
  the bag breaking,

I've been thinking: This is what the living do. And yesterday, hurrying
  along those
wobbly bricks in the Cambridge sidewalk, spilling my coffee down my
  wrist and sleeve,

I thought it again, and again later, when buying a hairbrush: This is it.
Parking. Slamming the car door shut in the cold. What you called
  that yearning.

What you finally gave up. We want the spring to come and the winter to
  pass. We want
whoever to call or not call, a letter, a kiss—we want more and more and
  then more of it.

But there are moments, walking, when I catch a glimpse of myself in the
    window glass,
say, the window of the corner video store, and I'm gripped by a cherishing
    so deep

for my own blowing hair, chapped face, and unbuttoned coat that I'm
    speechless:
I am living, I remember you.

Buddy

Andy sees us to the door, and Buddy is suddenly all over him, leaping
and barking because Andy said: walk. Are you going to walk home?
 he said.

To me. And Buddy thinks him and now, and he's wrong. He doesn't
understand the difference between sign and symbol like we do—the thing

and the word for the thing, how we can talk about something when
 it's not
even there, without it actually happening—the way I talk about John.

Andy meant: soon. He meant me. As for Buddy, Andy meant: later.
 When he
was good and ready, he said. Buddy doesn't understand. He's in a state

of agitation and grief, scratching at the door. If one of us said, Andy,
when Andy wasn't there, that silly Buddy would probably jump up
 barking

and begin looking for him.